5 Steps to Fabulous

Marcy,
We need more women like you in the world, so supportive, a true sister.
♥ U!
Keep being fabulous! ♥

5 Steps to Fabulous

Choices for Living Beautifully, Inside and Out!

Vanessa Coppes

For Tomás and Samuel…you are everything.

For every woman out there pursuing her dreams:

You *are* a beautiful, fabulous being.

Walk in Faith and everything you need will be revealed to you.

This book is

Rated

R

For REAL!

Table of Contents

Before we begin ...

Out of respect for my mother, who will continue to give me hell about this for years to come, I would like to apologize for some of the language I use in this book.

I curse.

I'm sorry, Ma. Please know that I tried not to, really hard. But, the truth is it just didn't happen. Not just in the book, hell not in real life. It's not too much, I promise, but guess what? I am human, and the occasional f-bomb gets dropped here and there. So there you have it. I confess. Living fabulously comes with a potty mouth included!

For every woman who has ever felt alone, ugly, fat, misunderstood and ashamed, who can't even breathe from all the shit in her head that keeps catching up with her—this is for you.

Let's roll!

“Owning our story can be hard but not nearly as difficult as spending our lives running from it. Embracing our vulnerabilities is risky but not nearly as dangerous as giving up on love and belonging and joy—the experiences that make us the most vulnerable. Only when we are brave enough to explore the darkness will we discover the infinite power of our light.”

Brené Brown

Introduction

If you can get past what you've been told about looking and feeling fabulous, and instead interpret all that information in your own way, a way that works for you and your lifestyle, the choices outlined in this book will not only simplify your styling routine but will also inspire and empower you to live more meaningfully, *everyday*.

This is not a book about how to dress or do anything *like me*. Instead, it is intended to encourage and support you in finding your own definition of what a fabulous life can look like *for you.* Because you are fabulous. You're a child of God and you do not need fixing. Maybe just some healing, like I did.

I have to begin by explaining how I got here. It's been a long journey, and as I sit here today, ready and willing to pour out my heart on these pages, I need to share with you where all of this came from: my life experiences.

I made the decision to share it all—and I mean all—because if you are able to connect with my story it may just empower you and help you understand that you're not alone in your journey. Hopefully you will be able to make the necessary choices to take action in your own life.

This book is the result of walking in Faith and allowing God's whispers be my guide.

Now let's be very clear. I have never claimed to walk around with a Bible under my arm (well, I did for about a year while I was in college but that's another story). What I do know is the power of embracing my humanity, my Faith and prayer.

I am on a mission to help women feel empowered and to understand that living fabulously is our birthright.

If prayer and meditation are part of your life, you can understand where I'm coming from. If they're not and you are still reading this book, believe me, there's a reason you're here with me now.

I'm sure you've heard people say, "I've been to hell and back." I've said it too, because I have, and I am sure you or someone you know has been there too. But I learned through prayer to embrace the journey rather than focus on the hell.

My name is Vanessa, aka V. I believe women are multi-faceted. We embrace our outer roles of wife, mother, sister, daughter, friend. We also have inner roles that need to be honored in order for us to be authentic, feel productive and be truly happy. We are artists, entrepreneurs, mentors and visionaries. When we ignore our true selves we experience self-doubt, anxiety and depression.

Like many women, I experienced my share of those negative moments. I struggled with my weight (anorexia and bulimia), had periods of insecurity and depression, with its new form after I had my first child, postpartum. Prayer, my parents' wisdom, and connecting with other strong, beautiful women reminded me how best to honor and nurture myself back to living life fully.

We all feel better and become our best when we embrace both our inner and outer roles (what I call the 360° Lifestyle).

I tried and I mean *tried* to separate my inner and outer lives, but finally realized it was impossible. If you try, you end up in a struggle that leaves you drained, depleted, unhappy and lonely. The healing process taught me to be good to myself because when I am not, those around me suffer, especially my children. I deprive them of my best self, the guilt sets in and I'm in a negative tailspin that doesn't serve anyone.

I'm sure you've heard the phrase 'necessity breeds creativity'. My parents didn't have a lot of money but they were both creative as hell. They did what any creative person would do, they taught us how to make the things we wanted but could't afford. My mom especially. That woman can still turn shit into gold. I am not kidding.

So of course, it was no surprise that I developed artistically at an early age—singing, writing, making jewelry, completing etiquette classes and mastering a make-up kit at 12. Heck, I even made some of my own clothes and handbags through high school.

I went on to study design in college and when necessity struck (the starving artist had bills to pay) I cut my design career short, got a scholarship and graduated with a B.A. in Education. I realized that as much as I liked making stuff, I enjoyed even more teaching others the skills to do something for themselves. Empowering others had been something I did organically. It became clearer to me that it would become my life's mission only after I started my jewelry business in 2009.

Family, love and an authentic life were the focus of my parents' lessons which to this day keep me grounded in my own authentic self. Both of them—genuine, kind souls and serial entrepreneurs—have been key to my personal and business success.

Today, my husband and business partner would probably tell you that I like telling people what to do. I simply have a keen sense of visualizing what women are capable of doing and helping them bring their dreams to reality; that fuels my soul.

We've been taught to make assumptions about other people's accomplishments. I hold a very special place in my heart for the very brave individuals who openly share their life's journey with others. It is a true act of courage to share your pain, your passions, your dreams. It is an act of courage to be vulnerable and let others see that we all feel the same things. Vulnerability is uncomfortable as hell and being vulnerable for me sometimes made it an act of courage simply to get out of bed.

My biggest lesson through my healing was that in sharing my story, I give others permission to share theirs. When you open up, you automatically break down other people's fears and as you heal yourself you set others free. Simple as that.

My personal and professional accomplishments did not come easily, especially when I attached their outcomes and my worth to other people or things. I fell into a rat race where the conversation in my head was, "If this person would just X then I'd be able to X ." And, "If I had X, then I could do X."

Can you relate?

The moment I realized that I needed to get out of God's way was the moment that my life became a testament to His grace.

Let me tell you something. There came the day when I prayed really hard for direction, on my knees, with snot and tears, pounding on the floor, pleading with God to take away the pain, the guilt, the shame. They say when you hit rock bottom, you will know it. Right there, I knew. And at that moment, light, calm, peace and happiness came into my life. In that moment I forgave myself and let God take the wheel.

My life did a 360° turn for the better.

So now you know my big secret: I believe in God and I act upon my Faith.

I get very clear gut checks whenever I pray. The really cool thing is, you can get them too. All you have to do is open your heart to your Source (God, the universe, a tree). This doesn't necessarily involve hiking alone in the woods for three days—although I've done that too and it does help.

My meditations are prayers. They are open conversations I have with my Source before, during or after my morning cup of coffee. I sometimes take time at night to sit and just let my thoughts wander onto a piece of paper. You may have read some of those prayers on my blog *VCoppes.com*. Prayer has become a necessary practice that starts out or ends my day with intention.

My intention is to be of service, especially to the women I cross paths with in this beautiful journey called life.

Chapter 1:

The Real Deal

Childhood, Abuse and My Quest for Meaning

Culturally, Dominican (Latin American) women grow up learning to obsess over their appearance. When I say obsess, I am really not kidding. I still have friends who do not leave their house if their hair isn't blown out professionally.

We are taught this by our environment, the people we associate with, the media, etc. We are taught that we *are* our hair, our weight, the brands we can shell out a pretty penny for. We are taught that everyone else is beautiful, not what you see in your own mirror.

Girls are taught to nip and tuck as early as 15. A weekly blowout is a strict regimen on every woman's agenda and even if you can't afford it, you find a way because you better look good!

Imagine that kind of pressure on a 13 year old girl. It's all bullshit, but at 13, it was on!

Here's *my* memory at 13...

I was sexually abused when I was five years old.

The details of what actually happened are irrelevant. What matters is how it affected me.

At five, I knew what had happened in my neighbor's yard was wrong. But it happened in a yard where I wasn't supposed to be playing by myself. My parents had told me not to go there. I did anyway.

Again, I understood that what had happened was wrong but I thought I would get in trouble if I told. I wasn't supposed to be in that yard. So, I didn't say a word.

When I got home that afternoon, for the first time in my life I didn't give our nanny a hard time about taking a bath. I ran upstairs immediately and locked myself in the bathroom. I ran the bath water as hot as I could bear and I scrubbed and scrubbed and scrubbed.

I thought that if I scrubbed long enough and hard enough, what had just happened would go away. I also knew from experience how happy my parents would be when they came home from work and found me dressed and doing whatever I was supposed to be doing. I believed that if I looked pretty enough, my brothers wouldn't rat me out about being in the neighbor's yard, and what had happened would simply go away.

I put on a Sunday dress, combed my hair and waited for my parents to get home.

I sat and waited in our living room. I perked up the moment I heard keys unlocking the front door, then watched the knob slowly turn.

My mom walked in first and smiled. She looked proud; my dad smiled too. Hugs, kisses, compliments ensued. My brothers ran in to greet them and the conversation was still about how pretty I looked. We went on to have dinner. My brothers didn't tell on me and I let out a deep sigh of relief: Everything was going to be okay.

From that moment on I figured as long as I focused on looking good on the outside, everything was going to be okay on the inside.

Your exterior is a reflection of your interior. Think about it. When you feel like shit, well, you sometimes look like shit. But I got *really* good at faking it. So good in fact, I was able to block out the emotional repercussions of my abuse for 12 years. Yeah. Twelve years.

But that wasn't the end of it. All that shit came out later in my life, in ways that as an adult I can now comprehend. *That* wasn't pretty.

My first episode. In high school I was going through puberty, enduring shit from my parents' divorce, failing math but passing art and literature with flying colors. The boy I liked was of course the boy every girl drooled over. Not only was he cute, but he was also a good kid. He did kind things, making him even more likable.

Well, I was his friend and study buddy. He of course had a girlfriend.

When I was studying at his house one afternoon, he tried to kiss me.

I froze.

Then I pulled away, ran into the bathroom, combed my hair, fixed my clothes and waited in silence for my brother to pick me up and take me home.

I got home, locked myself in my room and cried myself to sleep.

I remember spending extra time on my appearance the next morning as I got ready for school. My hair looked great, my uniform more starched than usual.

I remember walking in and everyone staring at me. At first I thought, *Wow my plan is working,* but as I walked towards my classroom and was greeted by Study Buddy's girlfriend staring me down, arms crossed and stamping her foot, I realized the shit had hit the fan. The whole school knew what had happened.

The rumors were beyond ridiculous and in less than 24 hours I had become the school slut.

It didn't matter how much I tried to defend myself, Study Buddy let me take the fall.

I was dying from embarrassment, in disbelief about the lies kids made up. I was 13 years old and literally felt like my life was over.

I felt naked and ashamed. I was so vulnerable I went back to feeling like my five year old self.

But, this time my reaction to the world was very different.

Chapter 2:

Healing:

The Work That Moves You Forward

This high school drama prompted me to tell my parents about what had happened to me that day in the neighbor's yard.

I could see the sadness in their eyes, and questions. How it had happened, when, where, why, who? I wanted to protect them from feeling the way they did. But I also wanted to feel protected. I could not deal with all this shit (blame, shame) on my own. Not any more.

The memory haunted me.

Telling my parents took me back to 7 years earlier and for about two weeks I stopped talking, eating or sleeping. I contemplated taking a bottle of pills or slitting my wrists. Frankly, all I wanted to do was disappear.

My second episode. The shame was unreal. I felt like I carried this huge label on my back that read "there goes the abused girl, there goes that slut." I was a bad girl.

Naturally I did what a bad girl would do: I acted like one.

I had become very good at lying about how I felt, and since speaking up for myself was scary as fuck, I spoke up for others. I got really good at that. In a sense, I was reflecting what I wanted someone else to do for me.

But I rebelled, against my parents, brothers, family, teachers and I alienated myself from my friends. My self-esteem sank so far, I felt both empty and worthless.

I felt dirty and ashamed. So I deflected anger all the time. I started smoking and drinking and of course, yo-yo dieting, abusing laxatives. I was craving and getting attention in the most negative ways.

I felt ugly. Losing weight and dying my hair every color of the rainbow and attracting men to my body pacified my need for attention. I placed my value in what people saw. Their attention felt like love.

I went through seven years of that crap. My mom knew something was up and she tried as much as I would let her to help me.

I was in and out of therapists' offices trying to understand what was going on.

Let's get very clear: By the time I hit 21 I knew better, but I *chose* to be with the people and in the situations that were bad for me. My actions were easy, desperate and misguided attempts to ease the pain.

Until I had my first encounter with honest prayer. It happened during one of those snot filled, floor pounding moments. My answer? I needed to forgive *myself*. Guilt and shame had kept me down. No more! Later I found this description of what I experienced in that moment:

"Guilt and shame are feelings that cause unnecessary suffering. While it is possible to feel guilt without shame, we cannot feel shame without guilt. The way to distinguish them is this: Guilt is the feeling that follows a perceived wrongdoing. 'I did wrong.' Shame is the feeling that we, ourselves, are made 'wrong' or 'bad' for what we perceive we did. It relates to the energy of every emotion from apathy through pride. Shame, on the other hand, is a grief-related feeling.

"Guilt plays a significant role in being unable to move beyond early abuse. When our parents, guardians, teachers, or spiritual leaders abuse us when we are young, it is difficult for us to accept that these people could do something so wrong. When we are young, adults—especially influential ones like our parents—have a tremendous amount of power in the world compared to our own. After all, they provide our food and shelter and are supposed to protect us from the outside world. Since we cannot yet survive on our own, discovering their fallibility directly threatens our survival. We may elevate the adults in our lives to the status of gods, or at least representatives of God. Therefore, when abuse occurs, we seek to pin blame on the only other participant that we can find: ourselves. We do this as a distorted, imaginary form of self-protection.

"Because survivors of childhood abuse often blame themselves for what has happened, many have been feeling guilty and punishing themselves their whole lives for the mistakes of the adults that they trusted. Once they release their guilt feelings, and stop blaming and punishing themselves for their abusers' mistakes, they are able to free

themselves of the emotional, mental, and visceral patterns of trauma and shame in which they've been locked."[1]

For 12 years I went in and out of the hell I had created for myself because I wasn't able to forgive myself for going into that neighbor's yard.

When you don't deal with the shit that happens to you in your life, it manifests in other areas.

As a child, I was unable to properly verbalize my feelings. When I was a teenager, and those feelings surfaced, they hurt like hell and I ran like hell away from them. As an adult I looked back at that five year old me and forgave her. I helped her understand that what happened was not her fault and that my guilt and shame could no longer continue to blame her. I was not the one who had robbed her of her innocence.

I now knew better and I had to begin healing and taking responsibility for my life.

If you've haven't read Don Miguel Ruiz's book *The Four Agreements,* you should. My favorite agreement is: *"Don't Take Anything Personally: Nothing others do is because of you. What others say and do is a projection of their own reality, their own dream. When you are immune to the opinions and actions of others, you won't be the victim of needless suffering."*

Now you may be wondering, in light of this agreement, how I feel today about my abuser. Well, here's the choice I made: He's a fucked up, sick asshole, *but* I cannot allow what he did to me to control how I live my life. I am very clear: No one should ever have to go through what I did. It caused me years of misery, pain and self destruction. And for a long time, it made me believe I was unworthy of love.

That was the lie I told myself, until I stopped believing it.

I decided to write a new story for myself. One filled with joy but most of all, forgiveness.

So maybe now you have a clearer understanding of why I am so passionate about helping women stand in their own light, and also

---

[1] Taken from "3 Lies That Bind Us to Guilt and Shame" by Hale Dwoskin

why I am so effective at making *anything* look fabulous with the flip of a switch.

The more I worked on this book, the more excited I got because as we've already established, in sharing your story you heal yourself and you set others free.

I spent too many years thinking I was broken and because of that I made bad choices. I pleased others, always considering their feelings and needs before my own.

Then I decided to face the demons in my head (the monkeys, the crazies, whatever you call them). And through prayer and *a lot* of self love, I accepted that I was a child of God—and God only creates fabulous things.

He didn't bring us into this world to suffer. He made each of us fabulous, discerning beings and when we choose to walk with Him we *will* have fabulous lives. Simple as that.

Here are the five steps I took that forever changed my journey:

"Our deepest fear is not that we are inadequate. Our deepest fear is that we are powerful beyond measure. It is our light, not our darkness that most frightens us. We ask ourselves, Who am I to be brilliant, gorgeous, talented, *fabulous*? Actually, who are you not to be? You are a child of God. Your playing small does not serve the world. There is nothing enlightened about shrinking so that other people won't feel insecure around you. We are all meant to shine, as children do. We were born to make manifest the glory of God that is within us. It's not just in some of us; it's in everyone. And as we let our own light shine, we unconsciously give other people permission to do the same. As we are liberated from our own fear, our presence automatically liberates others."

Marianne Williamson

Chapter 3:

Step 1:

Community C.H.I.C.A.S. and The Power of Connections

I have read hundreds of self improvement books, I've been to therapy, gone on spiritual retreats, attended hundreds of business and personal development conferences. I've practiced yoga, studied (like hit the books study) human development. I mean, I have been open to doing the work since my epiphany when I was 16 years old.

However, when I decided to share my story, I was scared. I was worried about what others would think of me. I am human, remember? Self doubt is a slightly dormant voice in my head that still pops in asking 'Who do hell do you think you are?'

I've learned to stare that witch straight into her eyes and say, 'Honey, please...get out of my way!'

I have not gotten here on my own. I've been blessed with an army of angels that have helped with my self discovery. They helped me get my shit together and when I could no longer keep up the superwoman facade, these Chicas stepped in along the way and had my back.

I define a Chica as a Caring, Hermosa (beautiful), Inspiring woman who lives with a Can do Attitude. A Chica is inside each and every one of us and whenever I need encouragement (even Oprah needs it sometimes), I still reach out to one of these amazing women.

These women (and a few men) helped me rise above those fears. They held my hand, wiped my tears, danced with me, taught me amazing lessons—and have walked in Faith with me:

Mami: You never allowed me to cry for too long. You always said to me "You can do it!" Especially when I was figuring out motherhood. Despite your own struggles, you upheld your strength, your voice, your desire to be and do better. I learned compassion and forgiveness from you. I also learned from you to see the person, not her circumstances. I love you.

Papi: My main Chico. From you I learned radical compassion for others, empathy, resilience. You always said to me "In any situation you're confronted with in your life, ask yourself, 'What can I do to make it better?'". This taught me to be proactive, not reactive. You also taught to speak up and show up for others who need a voice. I miss you, everyday.

Josh: I know you did not see any of this coming when we met yet you've battled it out with me every step of the way. I love you for loving all of me.

My Children: Tomás and Samuel. Your lives are sacred blessings. I've brought you along for this ride because I will not put you in the role of limiting or providing me with excuses for pursuing my dreams. You are why I dream even bigger and in color. You are my heart. Mama loves you!

My Brothers: You taught me, as the only girl in our home, to fight for what I wanted in this "man's world." The feminist in me thanks you.

Tias: A las Borbones le dieron un cereal especial. Esa madre de ustedes me enseño el camino del Señor y las lleno a ustedes de perseverancia, bondad y amor. Las adoro.

Uvas: Espero en Dios que lo positivo de este mensaje que escribo las ayude a tomar decisiones para su felicidad y desarrollo personal y profesional. Para que vivan sus vidas entendiendo que son capaces de hacer con ella lo que ustedes se propongan. Las amo.

V: Gracias por ser un amigo incondicional.

Christine: You sat with me in the freezing ass cold and helped me sell my jewelry when I started my business. You watched my kids and cheered me on. Thank you.

Debbie Coppes: Thank you for the encouragement and support along this journey. I love you.

Debbie Thacker Coppes: You were my first customer and you (and Justin) hosted my first jewelry party! But I don't think you know you taught me first business lesson: "Businesses don't run on free." Thank you and Justin for your support over the years.

Andrea Rosenfeld: Such a crazy story how we met. So blessed by everything you came into my life to teach me. Thank you.

Jennifer Tuma-Young: Soul sister. Not to sound like Dr. Seuss but you get me, I get you. You see me, I see you. I love you and cherish our sisterhood dearly.

Susan Vernicek: Supportive of my mission since day one. No questions asked. You are a rock star, Girl. Thank you!

Michelle Cleary: Woman! You turned my message into a beautiful song that I can listen to in your beautiful voice. Thank you for your encouragement and, most of all, your friendship.

Patty Lennon: The first mother in business who didn't look at me like I had ten heads when I told you how I felt about motherhood and building a business. You have made it your mission to empower mothers like me, who want to have outside lives and still be great moms. Girl, your words went beyond empowerment.

Jerry Amarosi: Thank you for allowing me to come into your space and share my craft. Your business insight helped me develop tremendously as an entrepreneur. Thank you!

Caryann Concilio and Amanda Intoccia: Your support brought enV Jewelry to a level I had only dreamed of. Thank you for the opportunity, your continued support and your friendship.

Francine LaMarr: My first business coach. When I moped, you didn't let me sulk for too long. You kicked my butt into gear. Thank you.

Courtenay and Daniel Hall: Working with you has been a truly wonderful experience both personally and professionally. Thank you for the lessons and the exciting opportunities working with you and BELLA have brought into my life. Above all, thank you for your friendship.

Lynette Barbieri: Everything happens for a reason. We were destined to meet and here we are on our ETTM journey together, empowering, teaching and supporting women to be the best they can be. I love you. No matter how much we pull our hair, our vision grows bigger and stronger because we know that together we can achieve more!

My ETTM[2] Community: Watching your lives and businesses blossom fills my cup every day. Thank you for believing that together, we can be the best we can be!

Lauren Baldwin: There are no words that could ever describe how grateful I am for you. Your support for me and my family has been invaluable. Thank you.

Maria Amalia León de Jorge: Lic...debo grandemente mi formación espiritual a su enseñanza. Nunca olvidaré sus palabras de consuelo pero sobretodo de motivación porque usted siempre vió algo en mi que yo desconocía hasta que camine con Dios. Gracias por formar parte mi vida.

Lary: Hermana del alma. Nunca tal vez sabrás lo agradecida que estoy tanto de tí como de tu mamá, estuvieron presente en los momentos más difíciles de mi vida. Love you more than you'll ever know sister!

Mercedes y Blanca: gracias por su amistad y apoyo incondicional, las quiero.

Natalia: Hija! Nunca me dejaste de animar en la persecusión de mis sueños. Esos domingos de mi vino en mi apartamento me sirvieron grandement de consuelo. Te quiero amiga.

Other amazing Chicas whom I have met along this journey and whom you should know about: Donna Cristino, Dixie L. Nichols, Claudia Chan, Lubov Azria, Latham Thomas, Agapi Stassinopaulos, Gabrielle Bernstein, Milagros Fernandez and Pilar Selman. Thank you for being fabulous!

"My ability to get through my day greatly depends on the relationship that I have with other women...We have to be able to champion other women. We have to root for each other's successes and not delight in one another's failures."
Michelle Obama, First Lady

---

[2] ETTM is short for Entrepreneurial Think Tank for Moms, an in-person and online networking group for women entrepreneurs. The group's mission is to connect local small business owners to each other, educate our members by creating personal and professional development programs, while serving as a hub for giving back to our community. Learn more: *EThinkTankForMoms.com*

Chapter 4:

Step 2:

Health: Take care of your body

You have to do the work both inside and out.

I had to get my shit together internally—spiritually—so I could project that love and compassion externally.

Depression is no joke and postpartum is not any prettier. Shortly after the birth of my first son, I felt like crap *every. single. day*.

Covering up how I felt was of course very easy for me. I didn't want my husband or family to think I would hurt my child. How I felt had absolutely nothing to do with him; it had everything to do with feeling like I had lost myself, again.

Being in baby mode 24/7 was not exactly what I had envisioned for myself at this point in my life. I had a wonderful job I could go back to, I had dreams for my future, but it felt like those dreams had taken a back seat.

However, God always has a bigger dream for you than you have for yourself. Little did I know that those feelings of insecurity as a mother would ignite the raging fire I have within me for supporting and inspiring women, mothers especially, who feel or have felt the same way I did.

I wanted desperately to show up for my spouse and my then 10 month old child. I *had* to flip the funk.

One of those snot filled mornings, I had errands to run. I had to get information about my son's christening so the stop at my church was on my list.

That morning, the office that I had to go into was filled with women and children. I immediately began asking what the meeting was about. One woman quickly interjected, "Oh this is heaven! We come here to connect with other moms. Being home gets lonely sometimes, so we meet here every Wednesday. There are volunteers who watch the kids right next door. You're more than welcome to join us."

Tomás and I became regulars and after several weeks of attending this group, those amazing women encouraged me to launch my jewelry business.

The message was very clear: I get to choose how I feel every day. I decide what to do with where God had led me in this moment. So, with an open heart and willingness to be of service, sharing my journey with as many women as I could, I embraced my entrepreneurial spirit and dove in completely.

Answered prayer? Heck yeah! And so much more has happened since.

Today, I work from home most days and adding two small children to the mix, some days, I am just too exhausted to take care of myself. I know the guilty that comes with carving out time for self-care and putting myself on my to-do list.

But let's break this down a bit:

Taking care of yourself is not selfish. It's an act of self love.

I'm going to get scientific on you now:

- *Self Care Improves Your Emotional Health:*

Taking time to care for yourself reminds you and others that you and your needs are important, too. It conveys to others that you value yourself. This contributes to long-term feelings of well-being for you and for others, who learn from your example and benefit from your enhanced health.

- *Self Care Makes You a Better Caretaker:*

When you neglect your own needs and forget to nurture yourself, you are in danger of deeper levels of unhappiness, low self-esteem and feelings of resentment. Also, when you spend your time only taking care of others you are at risk for getting burned out on all the giving, which then makes it even more difficult to care for others or yourself. You'll be caught in a downward spiral. Taking time to care for yourself regularly can make you a better caretaker for others, especially your children.

- *Self Care Releases Stress:*

Giving your body some special treatment is a natural way to relieve stress. Spa-like activities such as massage and warm baths have been known to soothe even colicky babies like nothing else does.

These activities continue to be effective tools for relaxation as we get older.

I *love* scrubs and gels, especially lotions that smell so good, you can't help but think happy thoughts. My favorite body care line? Dixie Bits by Dixie L. Nichols.

You will love her story and her products! Learn more about it at *DixieBits.com*

Transmit Health from Within

Practicing healthy habits is one of the building blocks for feeling and being fabulous. You are what you eat, and eating a balanced diet will yield a healthier body inside and out.

Exercise can help prevent excess weight gain or help maintain weight loss. Regular physical activity also can help prevent or manage a wide range of health problems and concerns, including stroke, metabolic syndrome, type 2 diabetes, depression, certain types of cancer, arthritis and falls.

Physical activity stimulates various brain chemicals that will leave you feeling happier and more relaxed. You will feel better about your appearance and yourself when you exercise regularly, as your confidence and self-esteem rise.

Exercise boosts energy. It can also help you fall asleep faster and help you sleep more deeply.

Exercise and physical activity are also a great way to have fun! As a general goal, aim for at least 20 minutes of physical activity every day. If you want to manage your weight or meet specific fitness goals, you may need to exercise more. Remember to check with your doctor before starting a new exercise program, especially if you have any health concerns.

Realistically, I make room for three to four 20-minute workouts a week. I consider a work out:

1. A dance party with the kids while making dinner.

2. Running up and down the stairs while doing laundry.

3. Playing ball with them outside in the yard or in the park.

4. Getting on the treadmill or bike (when I am being really good to myself).

The point is to move. And when it comes to eating healthy, ditch the diets. Instead, eat for energy and for pleasure, both in moderation.

When there is an excess of anything in our lives, we need to dig a little deeper and understand that there is more going on. When you notice that you're overindulging, it's important to try to understand that there is something tugging at your soul. If you find that you're feeding yourself Fruit Loops for breakfast, lunch and dinner, be aware. Understand that you need to analyze why Toucan Sam is now your new BFF.

A lot of our internal and external tugs of wars are simply because we were taught that dealing with our shit is really hard work. And we resist. And *it* is hard work, because it's painful. But doing this work is the only way you can move forward. And that is *so* worth it!

One of your rewards for staying moderate with your eating is clearer messages from you gut. Years ago, I decided to interpret the intuition I feel in my belly as God's way of physically guiding me through life. I've always said that my gut is my compass. The more aware you become of how powerful your instincts are, the more able you are to use them as guides in your life.

In essence, when it comes to feeding yourself and your family, understand that moderation is key.

I highly recommend the book Balance *Your Life, Balance the Scale,* by my good friend Jennifer Tuma-Young. I recommend it here because while the book touches on healthy eating, it's so much more than a guide to weight loss.

Women of every age are obsessed with weight. Jennifer's book demystifies every women's quest for the perfect number on the scale.

Life is so much more than that. When you give yourself permission to live in balance, the one defined by your choices, the work won't seem like work after all.

Spend Some Time On Your Appearance

The main challenge I've heard over the years from other women is lack of time, money and/or interest to style or groom themselves. Yet we *will* spend an average of $12,000 a year on beauty/grooming products and services.

A little ironic, don't you think?

Taking the time to choose clothes that compliment your body type and shape, and selecting accessories to accentuate your features, ensures that you feel good about yourself. When you feel good, you project a more beautiful you.

My biggest lesson: Embrace your body and fall in love with a brand that works for you.

Apple, pear, orange? These are fruits, not body shapes. We've been taught to believe that we have to be a certain shape or size in order to look good. I'm calling bullshit.

You are here and you are beautiful. Your body is a temple and you should treat it as a temple no matter what size you wear. Your size is just a number. It does not define you.

I've been many different sizes in my life and I've learned which parts of my body I like to accentuate and which I'd prefer to leave unnoticed. Here are some tips to help you learn how to do both:

- Clothes

Instead of shopping for clothes at random stores and then getting home just to look in your closet and still say, "I have nothing to wear," take some time to learn the sizes and cuts of a specific brand that look good on you. This will cut down on shopping time and your stress level when trying to find an outfit.

There's a lot of noise out there coming from the different stores and advertisements that make you feel like you have to go out and buy the latest 'whatever.' Shut it out by knowing *absolutely* what works on you and what doesn't. Trends pass but your style can be developed.

- Jewelry

Jewelry is a way to enhance your look by drawing attention to different parts of your body. Believe it or not, your body type could help you choose your jewelry and therefore help you make the most of the pieces you buy.

I firmly believe that a great piece of jewelry compliments your entire look. Most of the time I wear solid colors (I pick classic pieces that I can use throughout the year). It's easier (and less expensive) to change a piece of jewelry than it is an entire wardrobe. And when it comes to choosing the right pieces of jewelry for yourself, your body can make decision making easier, saving you time and money.

Here are some great tips to follow when purchasing jewelry:

1. Women characterized by a smaller bust-line, sloping shoulders, full hips and a small waist should always try to draw attention away from the lower part of their body and to make the bust appear bigger. One way is to wear a chunky necklace that would draw attention upwards and will also highlight the top half of the body. Long earrings will have the same effect.

2. Women with round body tend to have a full face, full bust-line, broad shoulders, a somewhat undefined waistline and a flat bottom will want to draw attention away from their middle. Wearing a double or multi-tiered beaded necklace can draw attention to their upper body. The idea is to draw a lot of attention towards your face.

3. Women with a rectangular body have busts and hips of roughly the same width and very unnoticeable waistline. They normally have a thick neck and proportioned arms and legs. In other words, everything works for them. Choosing jewelry for this body type would be a matter of preference.

Visit *EnvJewelry.com* for more fun designs!

- Handbags

I love a great handbag! I can't do without it!

Believe it or not, some handbags can accentuate your body. I personally use handbags as a statement piece (even if it's serving diaper duties!).

A great handbag is an investment piece that can also make a $5 tee look like a $500 one.

Where our handbag meets our body determines where others' eyes will be drawn.

I've always said, if you're going to splurge on just one handbag, the color and design of your handbag should be versatile enough to go with more than one outfit.

Here are five ways to pick the perfect handbag according to your body type:

1. If you have curves, select a small purse with a short strap. This type tucks in nicely under the arm, draws the observer's eye upward, and doesn't add any layers to the lower half of your body.
2. If your 'girls' are the life of the party, choose a larger bag with a longer strap to take attention away from your bosom.
3. For a thin and sleek body, a large bag will work perfectly.
4. If you're fuller underneath the waist, a smaller bag with a hint of color or a subtle pattern, one with a short to medium length strap, will work best for you. This keeps the focus on the upper half of your body.
5. For the hourglass body, anything goes!

- Shoes

I once owned over 200 pairs of shoes. Say what?!? Yeah, I know. I love shoes because they easily make you feel like a million bucks. They can make your outfit *look* like a million bucks too. My advice: Wait for sales on high end brands but make it a point to invest in at least the following:

1. Ballerina flats.
2. Classic black heels.
3. A wedged sandal.
4. A flat sandal

Like the saying, "Keep your standards and heels high," high heels will always help you look and feel fabulous!

See how it works? Once you've spent time and money on your outfit, maximize it by taking the time to pick the very accessories for the outfit *and* your body type and shape.

• Your Skin

This has been one of my biggest dilemmas throughout my entire life. I've suffered from severe acne since my teen years. And I've learned that a good skin care routine is really important if you want healthy skin.

When it comes to developing a routine that optimizes the health of your skin, there are many things to consider. With products for every type of skin, it can be difficult to identify which one is right for you.

First, identify what kind of skin you have. Is it dry or oily, light or dark, wrinkled or smooth, or somewhere in between? Ingredients in each skin care product should be tailored to meet the needs of your skin type. There are three basic skin types: dry, oily and combination/normal.

No matter what your skin type, the basic steps of a good skin care routine are the same:

1. Cleanse. You will most likely need to wash your face only in the morning and before bed, no matter what type of skin you have.

2. Moisturize. Moisturizer is a must for dry skin. The drier the skin, the more moisturizing ingredients your moisturizer should contain. Use moisturizer when the skin is still damp. This helps the skin lock in extra moisture. Only use as much moisturizer as you need. Over-moisturizing can cause clogged pores, leading to breakouts.

3. Repair. After cleansing and moisturizing, your skin care routine should be tailored to the specific conditions that affect your skin. Finding a product that is right for your skin can greatly improve its appearance and condition. So take time to experiment.

4. Prevent. A good skin care routine isn't just about looking good for the day. It's also about setting yourself up for life. Taking the proper steps to promote both short- and long-term skin health is just as important as washing your face. Sunscreen is

an important product for everyone to include in their skin care routines. If you don't have time to apply many different products, don't worry. Many products address more concerns than you expect. For example, many moisturizers contain SPF, and many repairing products contain the same ingredients that will prevent future skin problems. Read labels to find out how many aspects of your routine you can address with each product.

Make sure you are getting the best possible products for your individual concerns. Don't slack. Your skin will thank you later.

- Makeup

Did you know that wearing an appropriate amount of makeup represents an attention to detail? Wearing makeup is important because it will positively affect the perception others will have about you, especially in a professional environment.

What I mean by this quite frankly is that it shows others that you love and care about yourself enough that you took the time to take care of *you*. And people respect that you respect yourself.

Any woman who tells me she doesn't have time, well, for her and everyone else, here are four easy steps to help enhance your features:

1. Have your brows professionally shaped. Seriously. Don't cut corners with this. You can then use a brow pencil or shadow to help fill in faint gaps, give symmetry to your face and frame your eyes.

2. Use eyeliner and mascara to define the shape of your eyes, helping them stand out.

3. Apply a little blush to give your complexion a healthy glow and add dimension to your cheekbones.

4. Wear lip color to define the outline of your lips.

Another one of the Chicas I told you about in the beginning of this book, Donna Cristino, is not only a great lady, she's also the founder of Jing Ai Organic & Natural Cosmetics.

Her makeup has dramatically changed not only my beauty routine, but also my life. I have suffered from acne since I was 12 years old, so using foundation and concealer every morning was like brushing my teeth. I wouldn't leave home without caking it on.

Since using her brand, I have not needed to use foundation to cover up blemishes—ever! This has allowed my skin to heal and regenerate and has even given me a healthy, sun kissed glow.

Jing Ai has truly changed not only my beauty routine but also my life and I want you to know about the company and my friend, the founder!

You can learn more about Donna and her fabulous products at *JingAiSkin.com*.

The Power of a Red Lip

Red is one of those colors that works well with every skin tone. There's just something about red lips that instantly makes a woman feel empowered, sexy, and fabulous.

When you think of classic red lips, who do you think of? I see Gwen Stefani, Christina Aguilera (and, yes, Marilyn Monroe) but I also see *me.*

If those ladies can be brave enough to wear red lipstick, so can I. And so should *you!*

Red lips help you release your inner Chica. Sure, not every shade of red will work with your skin tone, so take your time selecting your best shade. Here are two tips to help:

1. Keep your skin tone and undertone in mind. If you have pink undertones, go for lipstick shades with a pink tone like berry or brick reds. Also, try on reds with blue and plum tones. If you have a yellow base skin, warm tomato reds with a brown base will work best.

There's just something about red lipstick that instantly makes a woman feel empowered, sexy and fabulous!

(Still confused? If you are not sure of what your undertone shade is, visit your local cosmetic counter and they'll help you.)

2. Keep the rest of your makeup neutral. No heavy eye shadow. Simply outline your eyes and add mascara.

Now that you know how to rock the look, you're ready to face the world as the fabulous Chica you are!

Natural Beauty Tricks That Really Work

Today, the most fabulous beauty fixes come from the most surprising places. What's also wonderful is that spa treatments are taking their instructions from good old-fashioned home remedies. The best part: There's science to back up the ingredients' effectiveness.

Here are some of my favorites:

1. Oatmeal: Soothing and anti-inflammatory, oatmeal contains beta glucan, a soluble fiber that creates a thin, moisture-retaining film on the surface of the skin.

2. Avocado Oil: Abundant fatty acids help balance skin's moisture levels, and the antioxidant vitamins A, C, and E protect skin from further damage.

3. Oranges: The fruit acid loosens dead skin cells. Cut in half and sprinkle with some brown sugar and you've got yourself an amazing scrub.

4. Milk: The lactic acid in milk serves as a gentle skin exfoliant, while its natural fat content acts as a body moisturizer. Add a gallon of whole milk to a tubful of warm water and soak. It's a great alternative to sugar and salt scrubs, which may be too abrasive for people who suffer from eczema, psoriasis or sensitive skin.

5. Apple Cider Vinegar: Makes skin inhospitable to blemish-causing bacteria. Take a hand-full of parsley and soak in 1/2 cup of hot water. Once cooled, strain out and discard the solids, add a splash of vinegar to the remaining liquid and a dab on freshly washed faced. Store in fridge to preserve.

6. Beer: Use for a rinse. Yeast and hops help to swell the hair shaft and plump the cuticle, adding volume.

7. Sour Cream: This thick dairy product makes a moisturizing mask and gentle exfoliant, since its lactic acid (an alpha-hydroxy acid) helps speed cell turnover, brightening dull complexions. Natural fats restore skin's moisture.

- Hair

I have personally asked every hair stylist I have ever seen to give me three different hairstyles that I can do at home on my own. With the right techniques for shampooing, drying, and styling, your hair can look amazing and you can do it yourself. Here are some basics:

1. To minimize breakage, make sure your hair is thoroughly wet before applying shampoo. Use no more than a quarter-size dollop, and rub the shampoo between your palms first. Lather for no more than 30 seconds.

2. After shampooing, rinse your hair with cool water to seal moisture in the hair shafts.

3. To distribute the natural oils in your hair, bend over and brush your scalp and hair from back to front until the scalp tingles; then massage the scalp with your fingertips.

4. Towel-dry your hair thoroughly before using a blow dryer. You'll save time and avoid damaging your hair with too much heat.

5. Dull, lifeless hair can be a sign of a poor diet. Try cutting down on cholesterol and fats.

6. Wait at least 48 hours after coloring hair to shampoo it. Every time you wet hair you open the cuticle. Give hair time to seal in the color.

7. If your hair is prone to buildup from conditioners, styling gel, or hair spray, mix 1 tablespoon baking soda with your regular shampoo once a week. Rinse and dry as usual.

Investing in great products allows you to get that 'salon' look at home; it also saves you time and money—and, oh yeah, frustration!

Now let's put all of this together, because I like to keep it real. Pulling off this fabulous book cover took some serious work. The pictures are beautiful. Alina captured the concept perfectly but I looked like hell before the shoot. The process of getting glammed up felt good. Giving yourself some TLC does that.

This is what two hours of hair and makeup *plus* Photoshop look like.

My *DR Glam Squad*:
Milagros Fernandez (Stylist)
Pilar Selman (Designer)
Alina Vargas-Afanasieva (Photography)
Indira Sánchez (Make Up)
Christie Checo (Hair)

Chapter 5:

Step 3:

Faith: Define and living by your own personal belief and value system

I act on blind Faith. I am also very clear on what my values are.

We as individuals know how we feel about a situation despite outside influences (gut check). Defining what our own personal beliefs are and living by those values align the body and mind. Be authentic to yourself and to others. Don't be a follower of other people. Your gut, your Source will never point you in the wrong direction.

I was watching the Academy Awards one Sunday evening.

I had made sure the boys and my husband were in bed by 6pm! I rarely watch TV, but I am a movie fan.

I had also just been named *BELLA NYC Magazine's*[3] *Social Media & Marketing Director* and I couldn't wait to indulge in the all night treat of glitz and glam, lights and cameras, fashion and beauty and share it on our social platforms.

The Red Carpet event began. I loved spotting trends for hair, makeup, shoes, jewelry. I was in awe of all the beauty, as any girl would be!

Then at 8pm, the show really began. The movies that had been nominated, each a tough contender in its genre, were all great ones. The men were as polished as ever, and the women in their beautiful gowns looked *fabulous.*

During the show and through commercial breaks I would sneak a peek, though, then munch some popcorn, take some notes and go on enjoying my night. But then, reading through some of the comments on my FB news feed, my gut began to pull at me. I kept thinking to myself, "This show is about the movies, right?"
It saddened me to see that women my age and older would put out such negative comments about other women: *"X artist can sing, but she should lose weight." "X actress looks like she's high." "What happened to X actress' face?"*

---

3 *BELLA NYC Magazine spotlights the ideal that BEAUTY IS DEFINED BY YOU. Both print and online initiatives present an engaging and informative combination of the latest health, beauty, and wellness resources. BELLA strives to inspire its audience to discover the beauty all around them by showcasing professionals who share a passion for helping others identify and embody their epitome of beauty. Learn more at* BellaNYC.com

"This show *is* about the movies, right?" I repeatedly asked myself. But the comments went on, and on and on and got pushed to the top of my news feed because other friends and friends of friends were jumping in to comment even more on "how horrible X's hair looked."

The famous NYC campaign that my toddler so avidly repeats, "If you *see* something, *say* something," popped into my head. This was all making my stomach turn.

I had to say something, not to point a finger at the commenters, but in hopes of creating a shift in the behavior that I was seeing. Because—come on!—not only were the words being used harsh, but sitting back and watching, being a spectator to making fun of others, is just as wrong.

My high school principal would've used a comparison like this to explain it: "What if you were standing in a corner ready to cross the street and you saw some else screaming at an older person with a cane to hurry up and 'get going' or 'move out of the way'?" Wouldn't you say something in the elderly person's defense?

Then of course comes the question, "Are you hurt by these comments because they touch on something that happened to you as a child?" Well my friends, you know the answer to that.

I've made it my mission to encourage every young girl I encounter to love herself first. The noise out there to do the opposite is very loud. And when the mean comments are coming from adult women, it proves to me that as a collective we still have a lot of work to do.

As women, we need to band together and support one another, not rake someone over the coals because she's having a bad hair day, or isn't a size 4.

Being a woman is hard enough. And I have to think, what road are we paving for our young girls on the rise when we talk this way? Because, believe me, our girls are listening and watching. How do expect to break the cycle of low self-image, eating disorders or body dysmorphia in our girls if we are modeling this kind of behavior to them? We are the ones who teach them how to be happy women. e are the ones who teach them how to live beautiful lives.

So I said so, on Facebook. I didn't say it mean, but I shared my thoughts honestly. *"To us girls out there pointing out the 'flaws' that we see in other girls: their weight, their hair, their age, their makeup...then we wonder why it's so hard to be a girl."*

I was unfriended by several people, women actually. And that's OK. Yet I had other friends rally behind the statement, share it and one friend even paid money to promote it. The whole experience was a reminder of my own beliefs. Those who weren't in alignment with my values weeded themselves out.

"...We pray for revival. We pray to be used. Then we need to be prepared for the possibility that sometimes the road to his kingdom coming isn't paved with gold and the American dream but rather dirt and blood like the way to the cross was for Jesus."
Mary Ellen Glasgow Smith

Chapter 6:

Step 4:

Self Care: Don't Allow Other People's Shit Become Your Shit

I have spent *way* too much time engaging in what turned out to be other people's drama, in part because I've chosen a life of awareness and service. I've had to learn to moderate my tendency to become a player in someone else's show. For me, being aware, conscious and present is something I cannot delegate or outsource. It takes effort. Through prayer and meditation, living this way has become a daily practice. But there must be guidelines and limits to how and what I give, and what I take in from others.

As I've gone through my own personal experiences, I've found the words of the Dalai Lama to be very helpful. Here are some suggestions, based on what I learned from him, to help you become more fully present in your life:

1. Let go of people who come to you only to complain, gossip, fear and judge others. Make sure others don't use your head as a trash can for their garbage.

2. Keep your promises. If you haven't been able to deliver on a promise, ask yourself why you are resisting. Remember, you can always change your mind, ask for forgiveness and renegotiate the terms of the initial promise. The easiest way to avoid breaking a promise is to say no in the first place.

3. Delegate what you can, and dedicate your time to what you enjoy. We tend to waste time when we try to be in control of everything and don't give ourselves permission to focus on the things we really enjoy.

4. Give yourself permission to rest when you need to but also to take action in a moment of opportunity. Nature has different rhythms. So does life. Not resting when you should drains you of energy—but so does not acting when you need to.

5. Declutter your world. A disorganized space, or a space full of things you do not need, robs you of energy. One by one, pick up each piece of paper, each memory, even each of your dreams and decide whether you need to hold onto it, or let it go. Then take the action to discard it.

6. Confront toxic situations you've been avoiding. Draw back from 'rescuing' a needy friend or loved one, or extract yourself

from an abusive relationship with a spouse or co-worker. Tolerating a situation when you can change it only drains you even more.

7. Accept the things you cannot change. If you cannot change something, hand it over to God or your higher power. This is how you can detach yourself from a situation you cannot control.

8. Forgive yourself and others and focus on the present. Living in the past or in the future will diminish your effectiveness in the here and now. Don't let preoccupation with events that are past or haven't happened yet rob yourself of the beautiful journey that is your life. Your life is made up of every second, every minute, every day. And even more beautiful, you get to decide how you spend each bit of it!

I've also given a great deal of thought to the negativity around me. Can you relate to these statements?

"The economy is terrible." "I haven't made a sale in weeks." "My job sucks."

If you tend to talk this way, you may have become a victim of your own negative thinking.

Have you ever considered that maybe the only thing stopping you from having a life you love is negative thinking?

Let's get honest: It's not the lack of resources, or the 'uncool' mom you had as a kid or the other excuses we use to justify not having the life we want.

We all have reasons to feel bad at any time during our day. I get it. Circumstances change for better or for worse in a flow of events. Naturally, we react to those circumstances as we've been taught by our families and friends.

But you may want to ask yourself, how does my reaction factor into this? Your reaction is energy and energy is everything. Everything you see, sit on, feel—the sun on your face, your kid's laughter, your morning jog, prayer, a great kiss—it is all Source energy. It is the origin of everything and everyone.

You are made up of this same energy, and its frequency can be raised or lowered according to your thoughts, feelings and beliefs. Therefore, the frequencies you send out attract similar frequencies. What you put out, you receive. Make sense?

Each of us has an energy sequence: negative on the bottom, positive on top.

Positive energy includes: our brilliance, goodness, divinity, inspiration, love, passion, optimism, happiness and joy (our connectedness).

Negative energy includes: our anger, depression, sadness, guilt, pessimism, sense of lack (separation, not just from others, but from our Source energy).

We go up and down on this sequence everyday, depending on our circumstances. We may think or say, "If only I had X, I could be/do Y." The ultimate joke being that if we get happy, our circumstances will change to meet us.

You can move up on your energy sequence by shifting your energy to a higher frequency and opening up to Source energy (God; higher power; a tree). This connects you to your inspiration, spirituality and goodness. It changes your life immediately!

From the low end of your energy sequence you can't even think about doing anything you love, let alone muster up the strength to go out and find out what it is.

From the high-end, you'll get new ideas, tap into your light and inspiration, connect with the people you need to see, and get into the flow of positive energy that guides you through your best life.

So, how do you flip the funk?

The first step is to catch yourself and redirect your thoughts. Use positive affirmations every time you notice yourself thinking negatively. I love these:

- I am.
- My life is abundant.
- Wonderful opportunities are coming into my life today.
- Today is a great day because I opened my eyes.

I am notorious for using humor to approach difficult situations. Humor is also a very effective way to raise your energy sequence, making you better able to respond to any situation.

Chapter 7:

Step 5:

Generosity: Experience the Beauty of Giving Back

Have you ever received generosity that utterly changed your life? You can also experience this life changing energy through giving.

Sometimes we overthink giving. Mentoring others, helping in your local community, or simply being someone's shoulder to lean on are all ways you are of service to someone else.

There's this magical synergy that happens when you give of yourself. Not only do you feel better inside, but giving adds beauty to the lives of others. You show up for people, they show up for you. You support, they support in return. When you smile, nine times out of ten, the other person smiles back.

"Giving is a Result of Obedience: We shouldn't give only when we're feeling cheerful. Don't wait until you feel like giving; just give and watch the joy follow. The cheerfulness often comes during and after the act of obedience, not before.

God's Grace Gives Us a Heart to Give: As thunder follows lightning, giving follows grace. When God's grace touches you, you can't help but respond with generous giving. Open your heart to your Source, your higher power, your tree and you will be so filled up you'll have plenty to share.

Freedom That Comes From Giving: Another benefit of giving is freedom from too many things. It's a matter of basic physics. The greater the mass, the greater the hold that the mass exerts. The more things we own—the greater their total mass—the more they grip us, setting us in orbit around them. Finally, like a black hole, they suck us in.

Giving changes all that. It breaks us out of orbit around our possessions. We escape their gravity, entering a new orbit around our treasures in heaven."[4]

Beware of putting strings on your giving. If giving has conditions, then clearly that's not very generous.

You shouldn't measure what you give and you shouldn't expect a return either.

By the same token, when your giving is taking too much out of

---

[4] Taken from the "The Treasure Principle", By Randy Acorn

you, then you are trying to give more than you are capable of. If you allow yourself to be drained of energy, you will have less to give.

Who you are comes from how much you give of yourself without losing yourself.

In giving selflessly of my time (to me the most precious gift you can give anyone is your time), I learned that the act healed me as much as the other person. That beautiful synergy? We need each other in more ways than we'll ever know. We are meant to live in community.

I have learned that our ego is what makes this natural act of giving difficult for some of us. Listen, one of the hardest things to let go of is our ego. I am not exempt from it. I work on it every day.

I am sure you can identify when ego is acting up in others: those who always think they are right, who control and those who think and act like they are above other people. The truth is our ego affects how we interact with each other.

Deepak Chopra describes the three things the ego is doing all the time:

1. The need to control,
2. The need to be approved, and
3. The need to judge.

He adds, "Be aware of them every time they come up and decide to let them go."

I know that it may be difficult to do but I have found that meditation and prayer have helped me identify when those feelings arise.

Deciding to live fabulously is living a life seeing abundance, rather than lack, child like wonder and awareness all while being your perfectly imperfect self. I learned that I am under construction: Constantly evolving, growing, learning from myself and from others.

When you decide to go beyond your ego and the internal dialogue...you can reach a state of bliss and joy. The following has become my giving mantra:

Be *kind*

whenever

possible.

It is *always*

possible.

Dalai Lama

Chapter 8:
Awareness:
Make the Process Your Goal and the Dream Will Follow

The power of our minds amazes me every day.

Mental perceptions become a part of who we are, whether or not we are aware of them. They affect how we think, how we respond, and how we act.

They create our belief systems, our cultural mores, our philosophies and habits. And we carry suggestions over from our genetic heritage, from our culture, from our parents and other family members, from friends and those who aren't our friends, and from what we have read, seen and experienced.

We carry suggestions from our environment and from all of the various institutions to which we are connected, directly or indirectly.

Many of us tend to overlook the importance of tapping into a deeper level of self awareness.

I realize it's not your everyday conversation to discuss the challenges we face each day. I am aware that you don't get to work on Monday and say "Good morning (insert co-worker name here), how did you handle your fear of judgment this weekend?" I agree: *Awkward!*

But here's the truth: The more you avoid discussing and facing your challenges, the more you avoid reaching your full potential.

The truth is that those uncomfortable conversations, that purging of whatever you're struggling with, will only make room for abundance, growth and yes, joy. Get this: Self improvement and self growth isn't self absorption. It isn't a selfish act either. It's self love.

Here are some things to help get you on your away to living fabulously:

1. Keep a schedule. It is a very good idea to write down what you have to do each day. As you complete each item, check it off. However, don't feel you are completely bound to your list. Be flexible.

2. Make time for breaks and fun. No matter what your occupation, take regular breaks. Try to make better use of your non-work time to do something fun. It will refuel you and help you get done what needs to get done with a more productive attitude.

3. Accept the things you can't change. When something bad happens in our lives, we try to fix it or change it. Sometimes we can't. This sometimes leads us to spend hours moping. If you accept the things you cannot change you will be a happier person. Acceptance allows us to find ways to deal with these situations much faster.

4. Break the chain. If you have patterns in your life, take a risk, try breaking out of a rut and doing something different every day. Not only do you broaden your experiences of life, you open up doors for the future.

5. Face your fears. I started choosing to do something every day that I didn't want to do or felt uncomfortable doing. I know it's different for everyone, but we all have small steps we can start to take towards facing our fears.

6. Live for the now. Don't fall into the 'would'a, could'a, should'a pattern.' You know—that list of things you've been meaning to do. *Go do them!*

Don't wait for life to happen. Grab it by the horns and *make* it happen.

"For me, the path to success was never attaining wealth or celebrity. It was about *the process of continually seeking to be better*, to challenge myself to pursue excellence on every level. The question I ask every day is the same as it's always been: How much farther can I stretch to reach my full potential? What I know for sure is that it's only when you make the process your goal that the dream can follow."

Oprah

Chapter 9:

Live Fabulously:

The 360° Lifestyle is 24/7

These *5 Steps to Fabulous* are choices I made while on my quest for living more meaningfully and being more fulfilled. Together, they are a lifestyle.

I pointed out in the beginning of the book that our outside reflects how we feel inside. I also pointed out how good I became at lying about that and how miserable it made me feel.

The truth is that these five choices address working on your interior and exterior. You cannot separate the two. We all feel better and become our best when we embrace both our inner and our outer beauty.

After I began working with women, moms especially, their stories of their internal and external battles were all too similar.

I receive a lot of praise about how, with two young children, several businesses and everything else I have going on, I seem to have it all pretty much figured out.

While I am humbled by the validation from others, the truth is, I *don't* have it all figured out.

As The Tidy Tutor, Kathy Roberts, describes it, I am 'organizationally challenged.' I have *a lot* of help getting it all done.

We need to stop bullshitting ourselves and stop putting up facades based on what we think other people want.

I've been blessed with the privilege of working from home, in my PJ's some days and I *love* it, although there are also some days I am ready to pull my hair out. The stereotype is that by the end of the day, I'll be a frazzled mess because I've been home with the kids all day. I refuse to accept that looking like a crazy-ass mom is what God intended. NO!

I've recognized my weaknesses, so there are certain things I just don't do. I outsource certain aspects of my life and I no longer give myself a guilt trip about it.

I've learned that my energy, time and resources are better utilized where they are meant to be of service.

I know a lot of other women who simply can't work the way I do (although I'm secretly scheming for a way to change that). I get it. But I also know that I create what *balance* looks like for me. Me. No one else can do that for me. And I also recognize that I need support in certain areas of my life, not just for myself, but also for my family. And cutting the bullshit with myself is the only way to plow through it.

All joking aside and to my point: Perfection does not exist. Doing and being your best is all you can hope for.

My best does not include folding laundry. My husband knows that. Hell, my kids know that. (And now so do you!) And that is OK.

I'll take playing with my kids or meeting with another woman to strategize about her life and biz over vacuuming any day.

I made the decision to live my life in awareness: taking in the good, the bad, the ugly, the hurdles, the ahas, the dark moments, the laughs, the cries, the difficult conversations with others and with myself. I also made the decision to let my Faith in God lead the way. I chose to be of service to other women by openly sharing my lessons with them.

Living life exclusively for others now feels like dancing out of rhythm. It feels unnatural.

Every day you have the power to choose whether it will be a fabulous one. Every single day. Why live longing, waiting, wanting?

I am a vessel of God's love and grace. I share that with others as much as I am able and can only hope everyone, especially those closest to me, can feel and see it too.

Make the decision today to live your life and let your Source, your higher power, your God, your tree, guide the way. Life is a messy and beautiful journey. Take it all in.

I pray this book serves you as a guide to make your own choices. I hope it inspires you to understand that living fabulously is our God-given right. We can all live in greatness.

So, onward Chicas! Here's to living fabulously!

More Resources for Living Beautifully

Feed your mind and your soul. Here are some of my favorite go to's whenever I am in need of support and inspiration:

- Prayer/Meditation.

- Blogs: *VCoppes.com, EThinkTankForMoms.com, BellaNYC.com, InspiredGirl.net, IdentityMagazine.net*

- Books: A Course In Miracles, Words That Matter by The Oprah Magazine, Blindness by José Saramago, The Alchemist by Paulo Coelho, Verónika Decides to Die by Paulo Cohelo, The Little Prince by Antoine de Saint-Exupéry, The Giving Tree by Shel Silverstein, Emotional Intelligence 2.0 by Travis Bradberry, The Total Money Makeover by Dave Ramsey, Memoirs of A Geisha by Arthur Golden, The Looking Glass by Richard Paul Evans, Daring Greatly by Brené Brown, Wishes Fulfilled by Dr. Wayne W. Dyer, Balance Your Life, Balance The Scale by Jennifer Tuma Young, A New Earth by Eckhart Tolle, Mama Glow by Latham Thomas.

- Magazines: Bella New York City Magazine, O The Oprah Magazine.

- Movies: The Color Purple, Thelma and Louise, Steel Magnolias, The Princess Bride.

- Groups/Organizations: Entrepreneurial Think Tank for Moms, Enchanted Makeovers, IEP Youth Services.

- Conferences: ETTM's 360°: The Power of Connections, Mom Gets A Business Conference, Claudia Chan's S.H.E. Summit.

Contact Me

I would love to connect with you. Join a global community of fabulous Chicas!

Twitter: @VanessaCoppes

27175658R00042

Made in the USA
Charleston, SC
03 March 2014